This Book Belongs to

....

....

Step 1 : Cut out the sheet

Step 2 : Color the picture

Step 3 : Carefully cut out the picture

Step 4 : Paste on another sheet

For Parent

1. Talk to your child about scissor saftey. Explain that scissors are only for cutting paper. Nothing else also stress the importance of not walking with scissors.

2. Get a good set of scissors. It is best to start with scissors that have a blunt point, however, make sure they aren't too dull and that they are sharp enough to cut the paper.

3. Help your child correctly hold the scissors. If your child is left handed, be sure to purchase left handed scissors.

Start slow and remember

Practice makes progress..

Practice Lines

Practice wave

Practice wave

Practice Lines

Practice Lines

Practice Lines

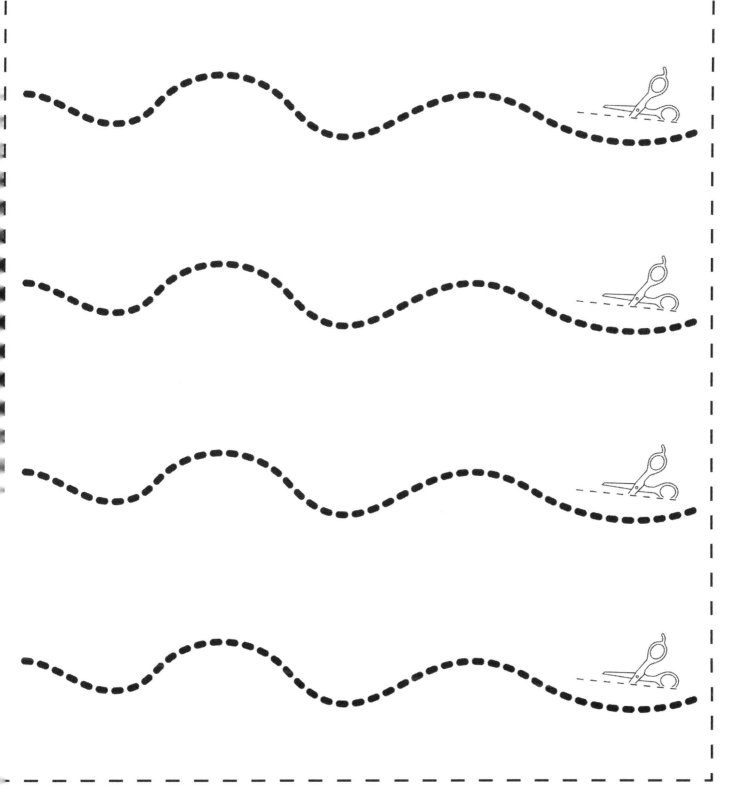

Practice wave

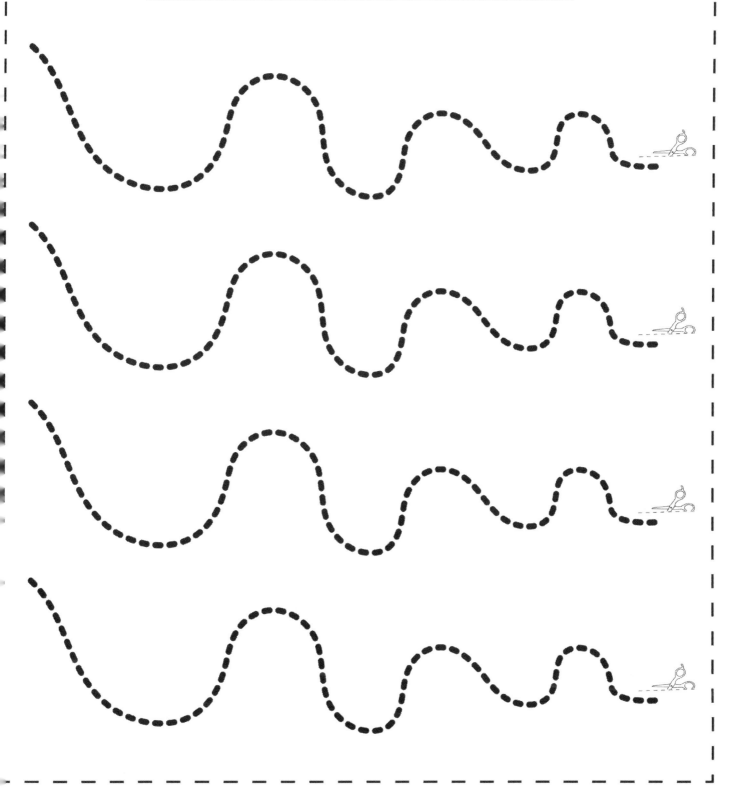

Practice wave

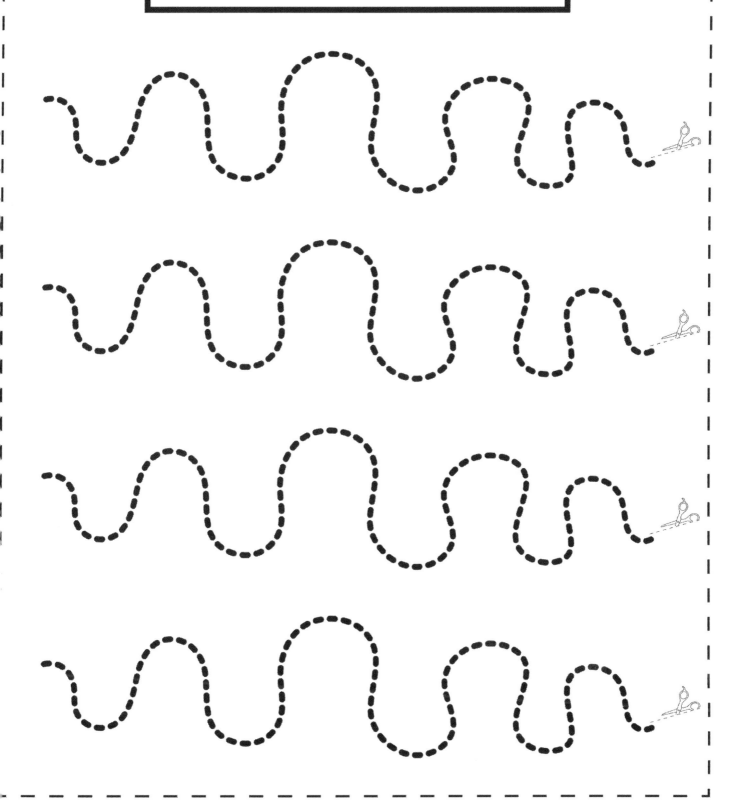

Practice wave

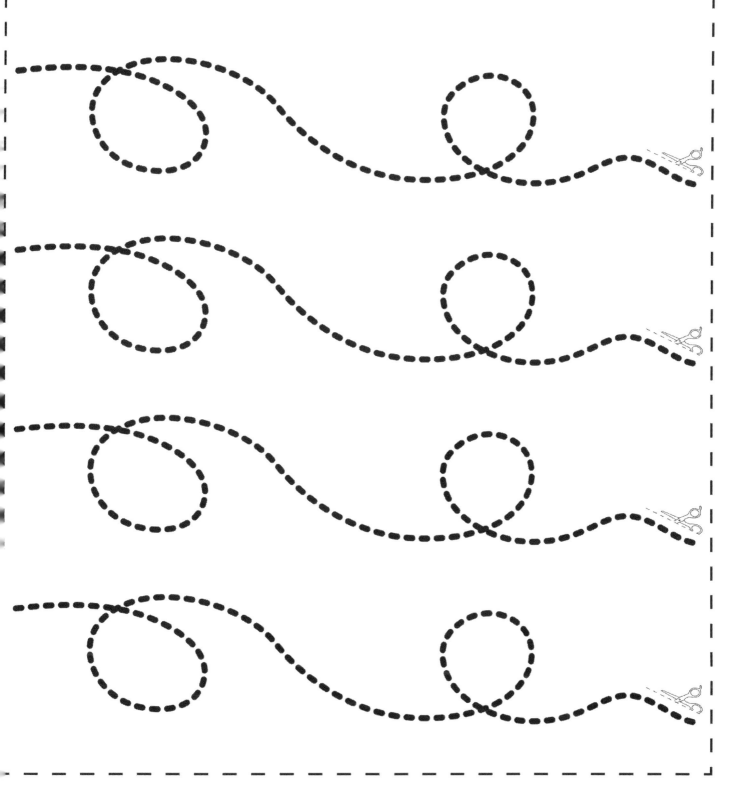

Practice wave

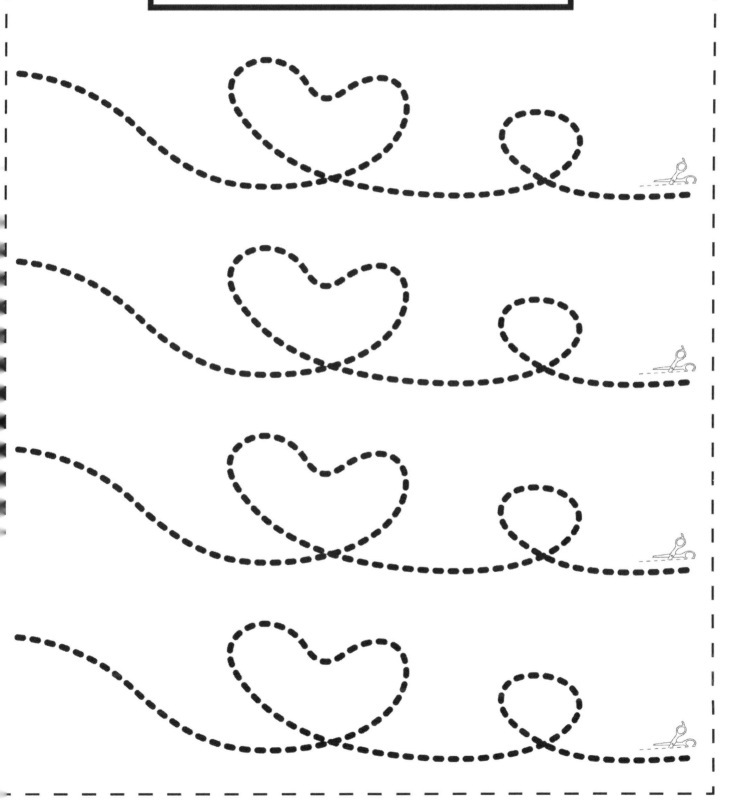

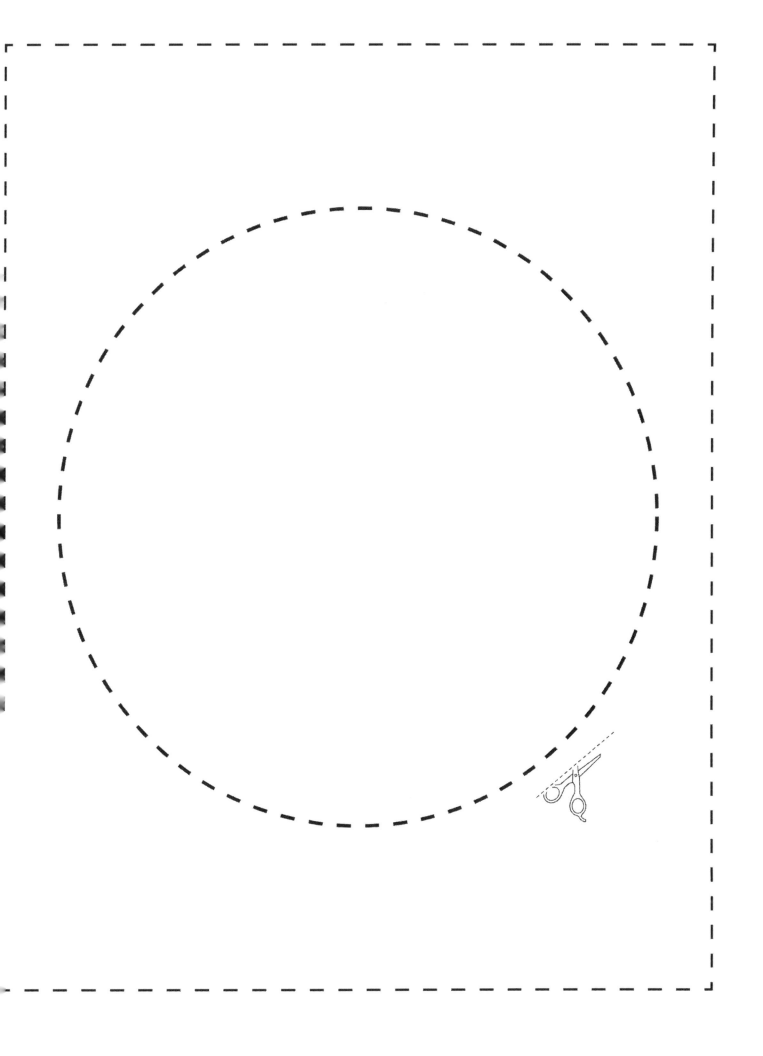

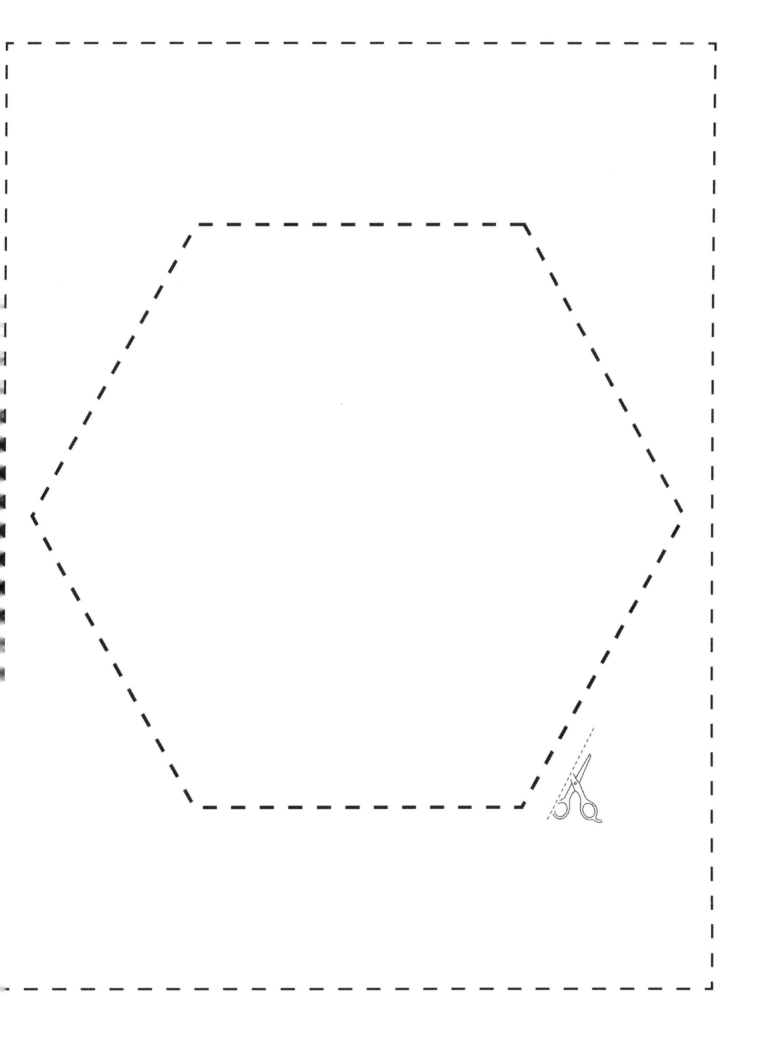

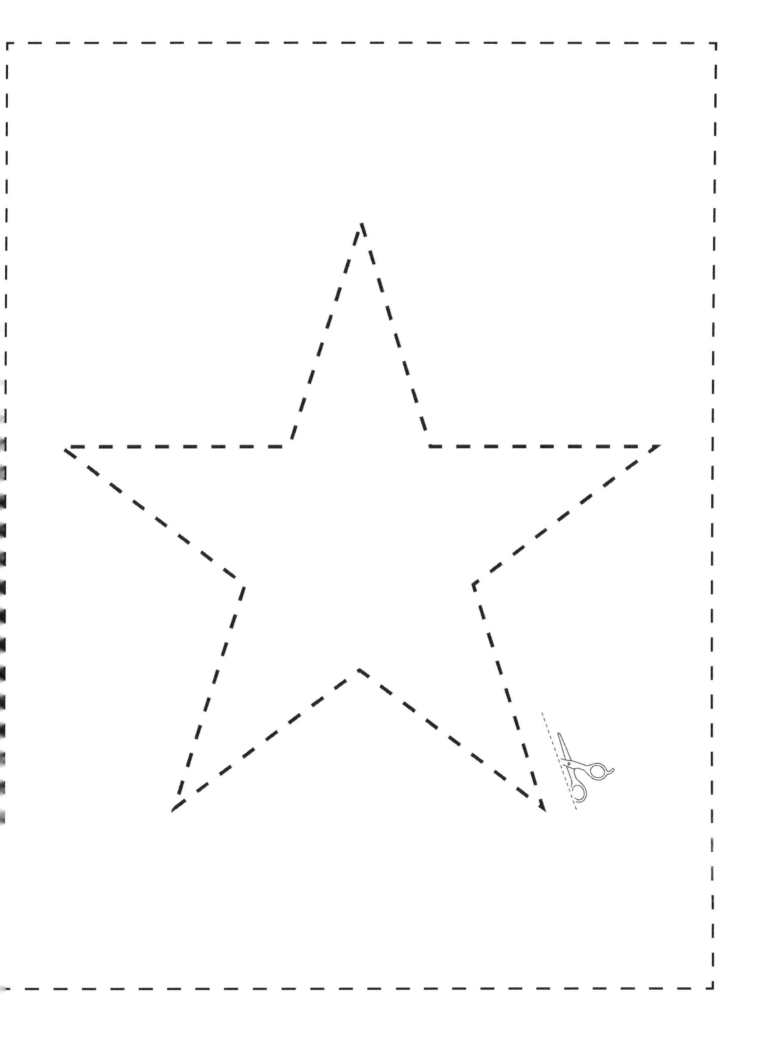

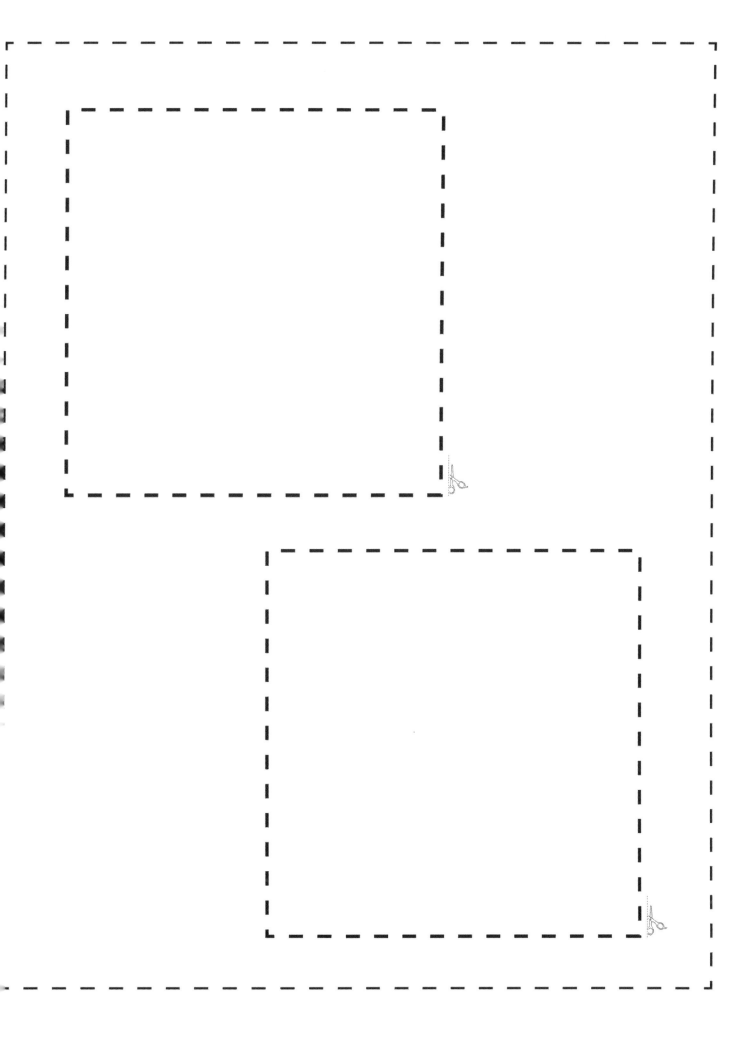

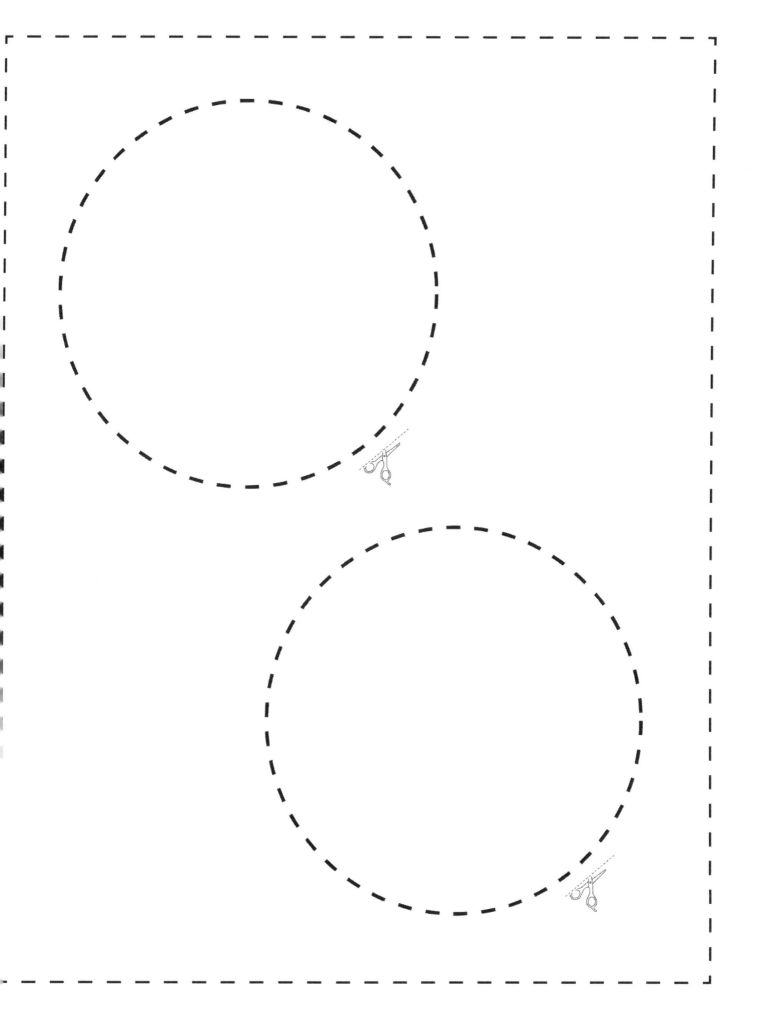

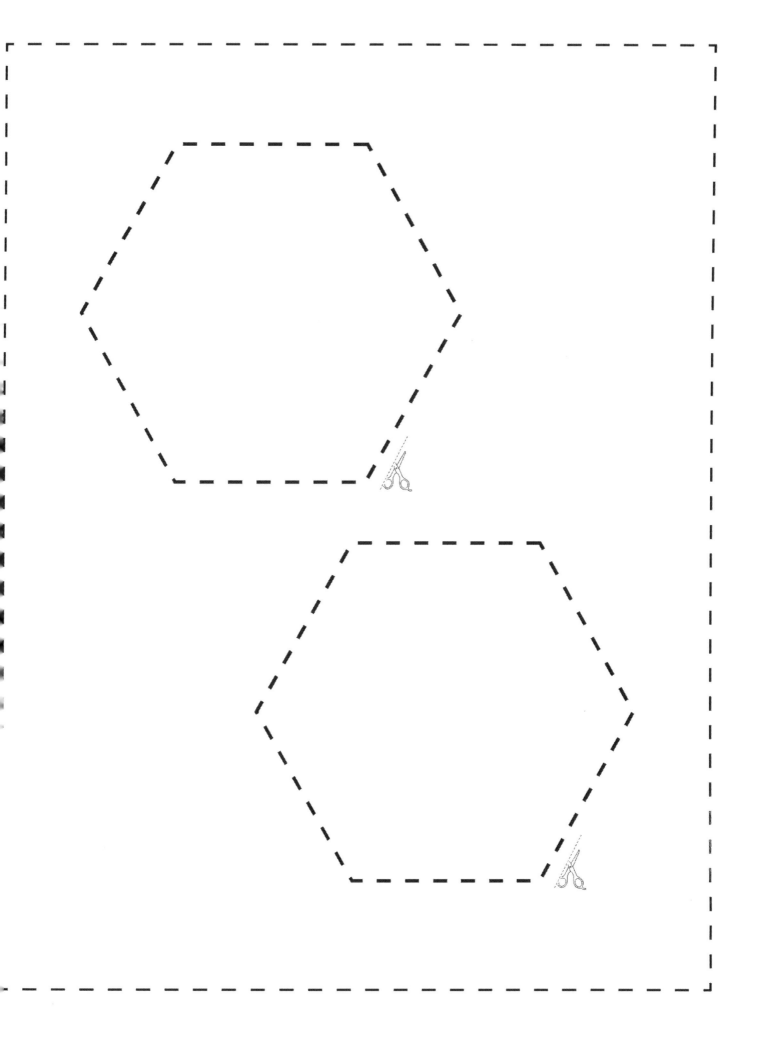

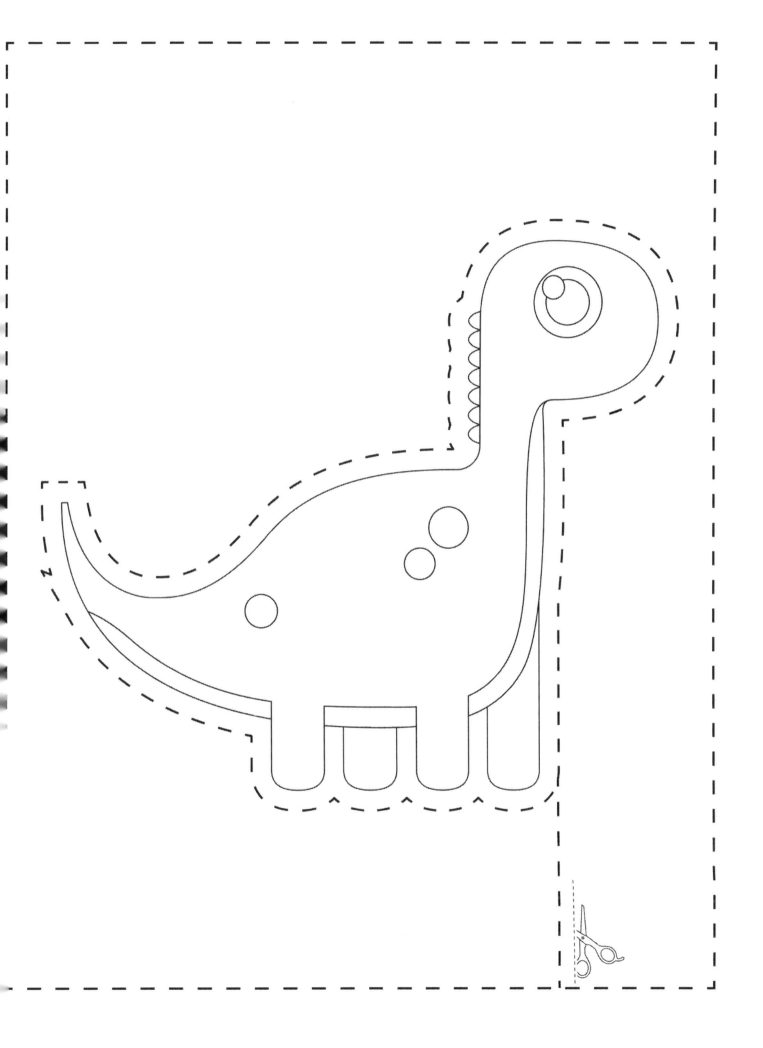

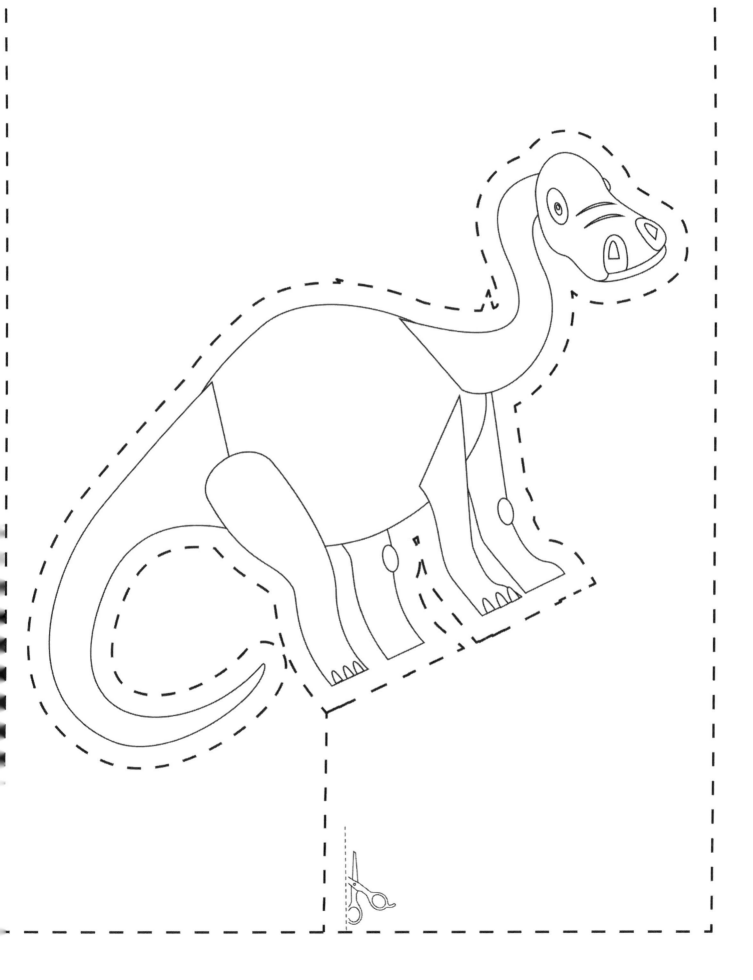

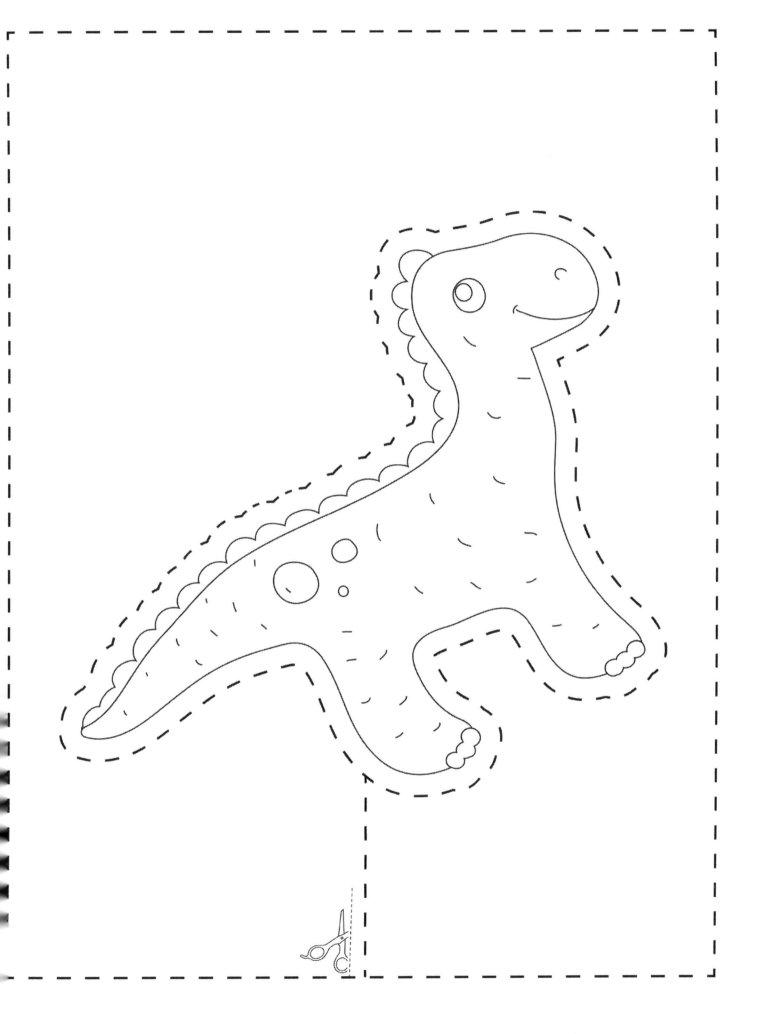

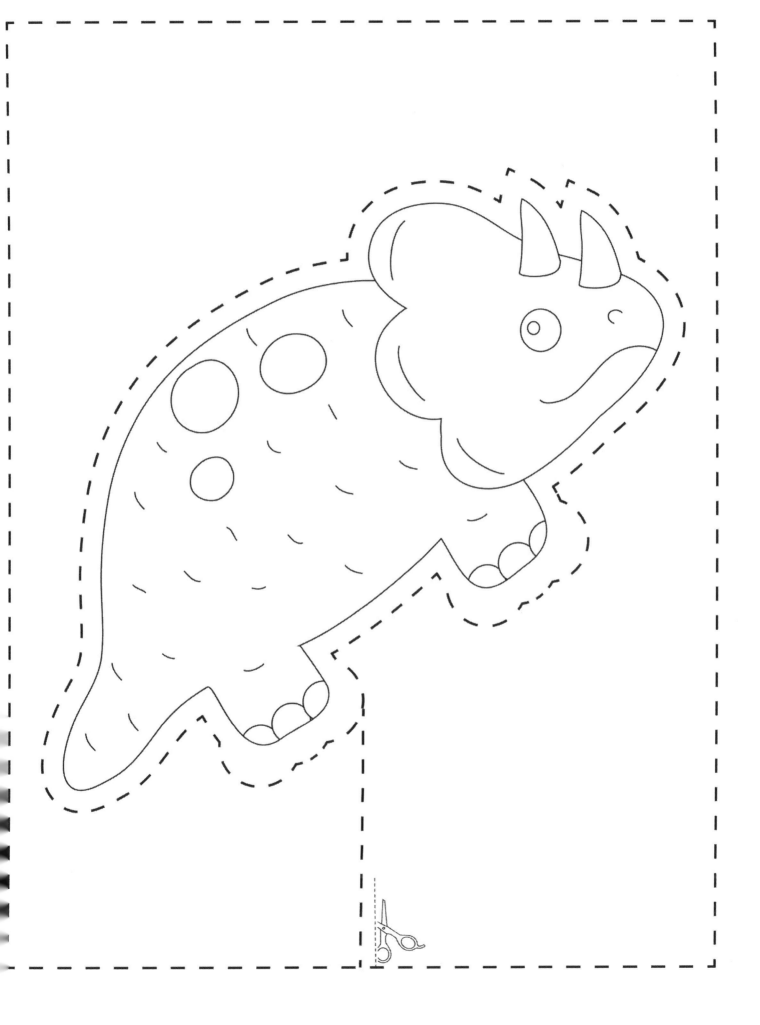

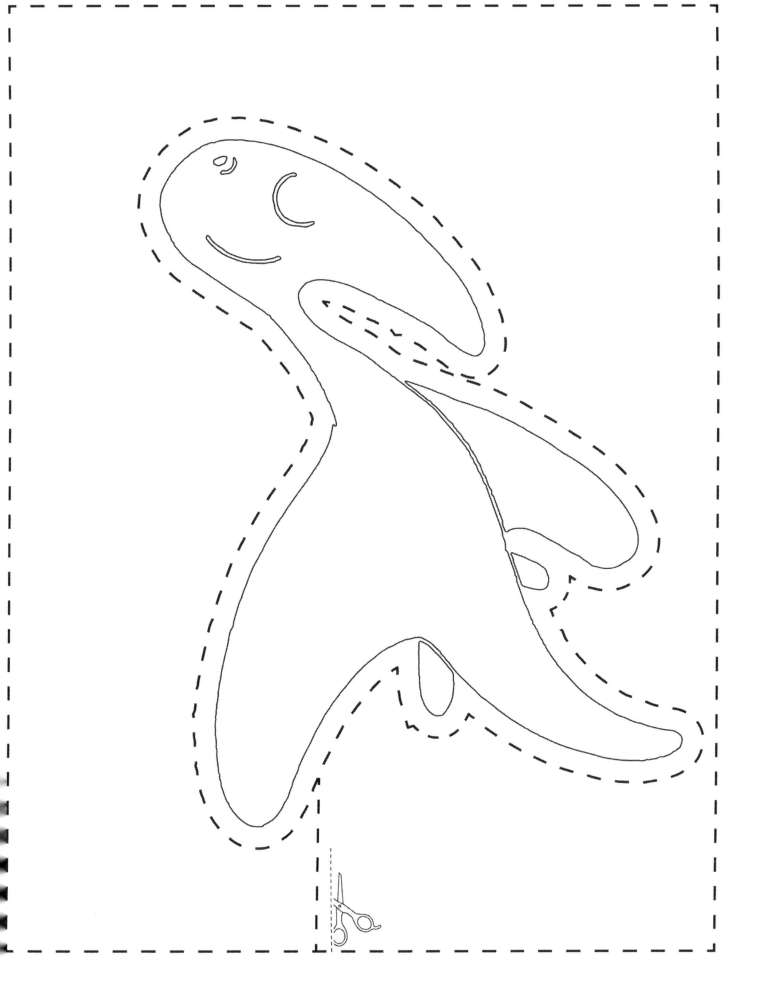

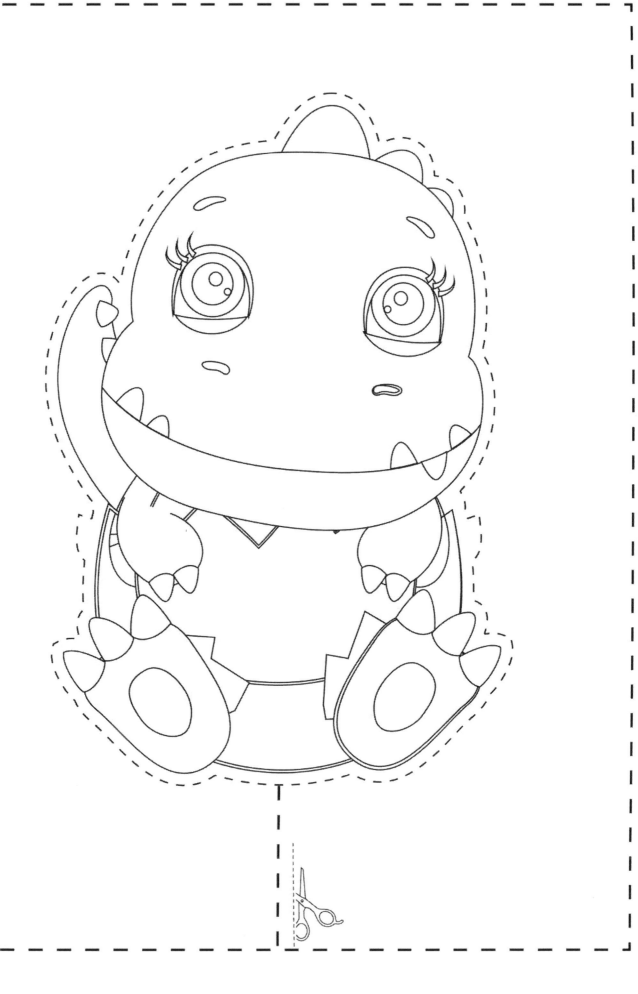

Made in United States
Troutdale, OR
01/31/2024